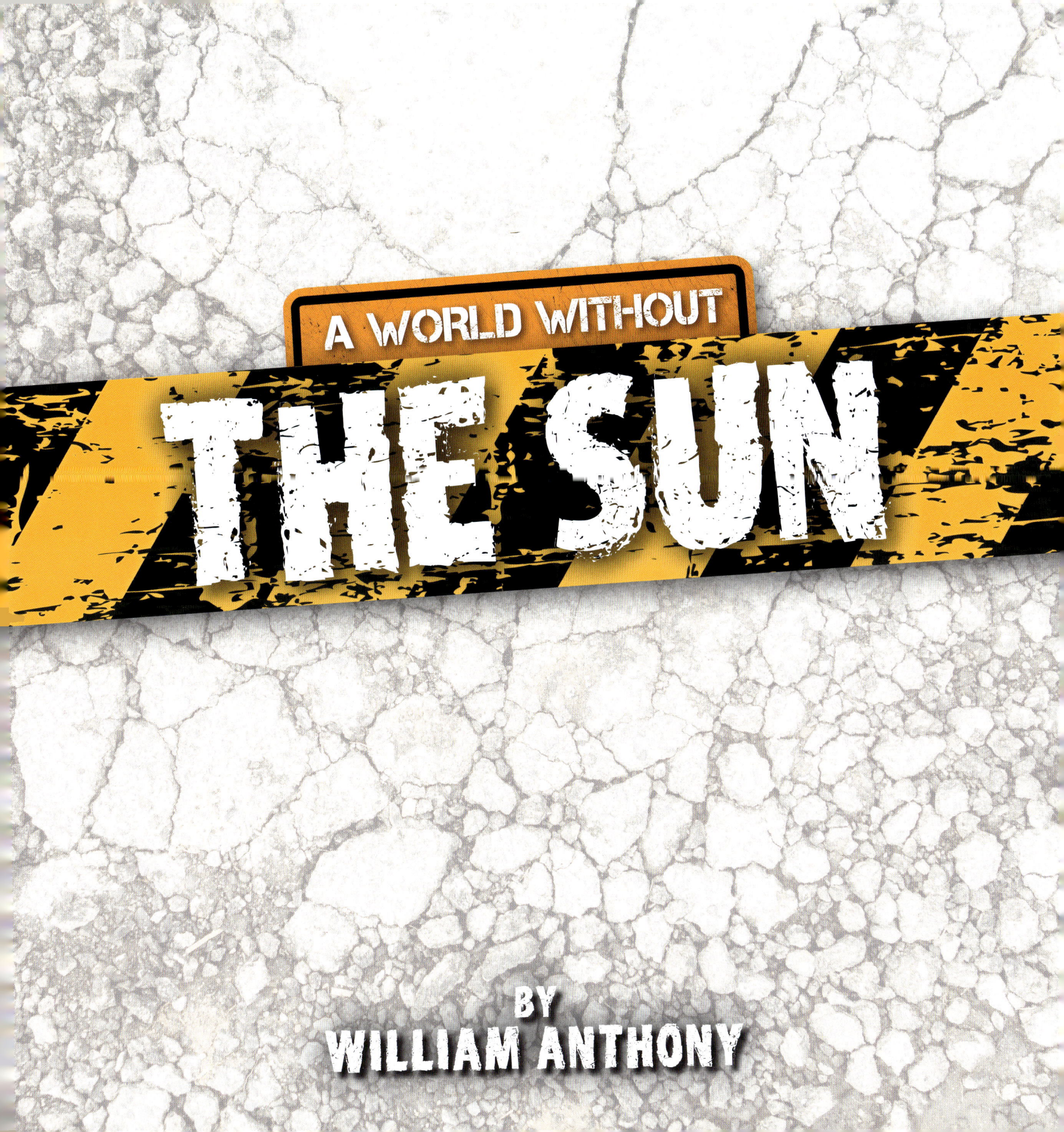

A WORLD WITHOUT THE SUN

BY WILLIAM ANTHONY

BookLife PUBLISHING

©2020
BookLife Publishing Ltd.
King's Lynn
Norfolk PE30 4LS

All rights reserved.
Printed in Malaysia.

A catalogue record for this book is available from the British Library.

ISBN: 978-1-83927-039-0

Written by:
William Anthony

Edited by:
Robin Twiddy

Designed by:
Drue Rintoul

All facts, statistics, web addresses and URLs in this book were verified as valid and accurate at time of writing. No responsibility for any changes to external websites or references can be accepted by either the author or publisher.

IMAGE CREDITS

4&5 – 3d imagination, Sebastian Duda, Amanda Carden, 6&7 – Gorodenkoff, Napat, TatyanaTVK, Aphelleon, Alhovik, panos3. 8&9 – Stephen Rees, Claudio Divizia, seecreateimages. 10&11 – barka, Monkey Business Images, LeventeGyori, txking, Kiselev Andrey Valerevich, CHURN, sirtravelalot. 12&13 – Rashevskyi Viacheslav, Alba_alioth, Harsanyi Andras, photosoft. 14&15 – Aleks vF, inxti, ESB Professional. 18&19 – Dima Zel, J. Helgason, Ural_art. 20&21 – PrimeMockup. 22&23 – Kateryna Mostova, StockImageFactory.com. All images courtesy of Shutterstock.com. With thanks to Getty Images, Thinkstock Photo and iStockphoto.

CONTENTS

PAGE 4	What Could YOU Live Without?
PAGE 6	Lights Out
PAGE 8	Have You Seen Me?
PAGE 10	Showing Results For: #Pray4Plants
PAGE 12	This Is a Public Service Announcement...
PAGE 14	Nearest Vent This Way
PAGE 16	The Prodigal Sun
PAGE 18	Brace, Brace
PAGE 20	Year 45020
PAGE 22	It Starts with Us
PAGE 24	Glossary and Index

Words that look like this can be found in the glossary on page 24.

WHAT COULD YOU LIVE WITHOUT?

Many people give things up at the start of a new year. Some people give up chocolate. You could do that, right? Easy? Who are you kidding, chocolate is too good to give up!

Could you live without any chocolate on the shelves? It's terrifying!

There are worse things to lose than chocolate. Imagine if the Sun disappeared! That would be very frightening, indeed. **DO YOU DARE TAKE A LOOK AT WHAT MIGHT HAPPEN IN A WORLD WITHOUT THE SUN?**

If the Sun disappeared, it would take around 8 minutes and 20 seconds to get dark on Earth. Unlike the lights in your house, the light from the Sun has 150 million kilometres to travel, which takes time!

The Moon does not make light like the Sun does. We can only see the Moon because light from the Sun is <u>reflecting</u> off it. Without the Sun, we could completely lose track of the Moon.

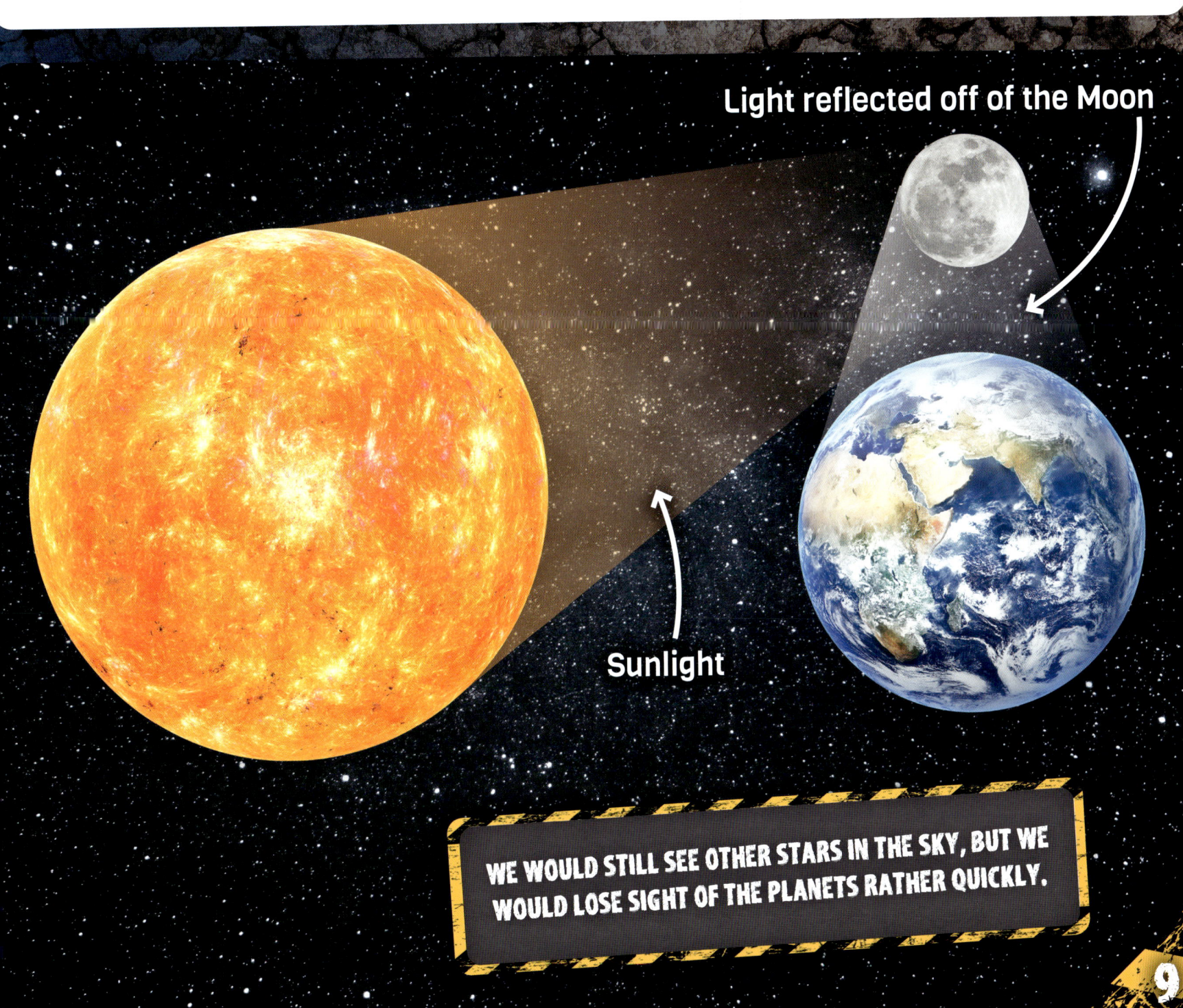

Light reflected off of the Moon

Sunlight

WE WOULD STILL SEE OTHER STARS IN THE SKY, BUT WE WOULD LOSE SIGHT OF THE PLANETS RATHER QUICKLY.

BECAUSE THE WORLD **NEEDS** TO KNOW WHAT **YOU** HAVE TO SAY.

SHOWING RESULTS FOR:
#PRAY4PLANTS

Plant Gal @plantgang
Yo, who killed all the plants? #WhereDatGreenGone #Pray4Plants

Greg Norbit @daffodils4life
Please put your hands together and #Pray4Plants (my plants are the most important, pray for those first)

Johns N' Roses @ThingsDieOnMyDesk
Wait, plants aren't supposed to look like this? #Pray4Plants #FloraNoMore-A

Say Hello to Vera @AloeVera
Sun gone. Plants dead. Toast burnt. Not a fun start to my day.
#Pray4Plants

Meme, Myself and I @ViralSharon
Carrot farmers did what? I knew Farmer Norman was acting odd...
#Pray4Plants

Plants need sunlight in order to make food and stay alive. Without the Sun, all plants would soon die. When we lose the last plants, all <u>herbivores</u> and most <u>omnivores</u> will die too.

Trees would survive longer than most plants because they can store lots of food.

Without the Sun to keep it warm, the Earth could reach an <u>average temperature</u> of -18 degrees Celsius within a week, -73 degrees Celsius after a year and -240 degrees Celsius after thousands of years.

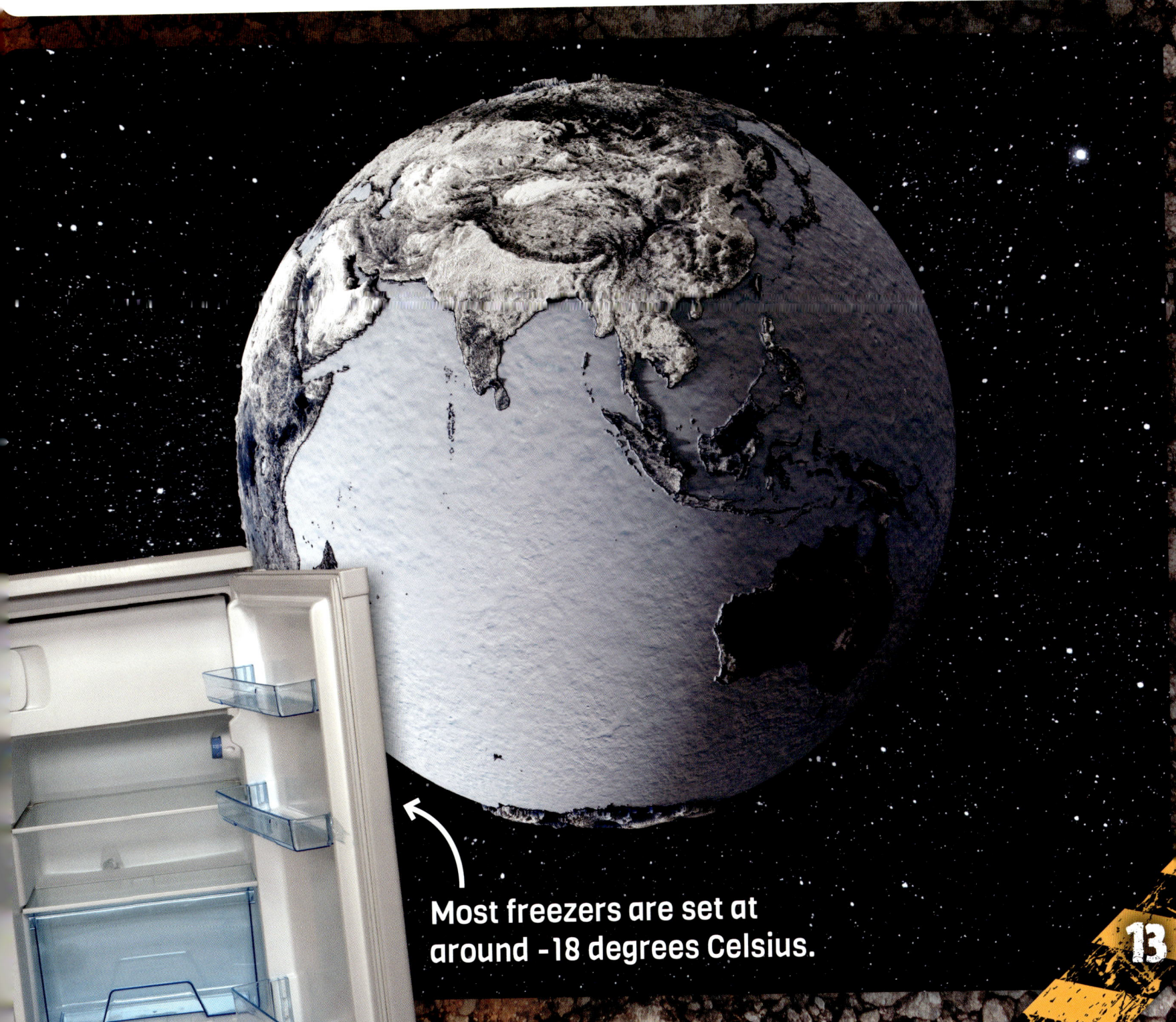

Most freezers are set at around -18 degrees Celsius.

After many years, Earth would freeze. However, like a frozen lake, the oceans would only freeze on top. To survive, humans would need to travel to an underwater hydrothermal vent – where heat escapes from the centre of the Earth.

We would need submarines to travel to hydrothermal vents.

Hydrothermal vent

The Prodigal Sun

MENU

STARTERS

Slugs	£5.99
Clams	£5.99

MAINS

Blind Shrimp — £11.49
with a side of blind shrimp

Crab — £12.99
with a pinch of pinchers

Octopus Tentacle — £14.49
with seven extra tentacles

Giant Tubeworm — £36.99
feeds four

DESSERTS

Assorted Anemones — £2.49 or 3 for £5.99

Most animals and plants would die without the Sun. However, some animals living by hydrothermal vents don't need the Sun to live. Animals such as shrimp, tubeworms and clams would be some of the only food available to humans.

WHAT WOULD YOU ORDER AT THE PRODIGAL SUN?

The Daily Goose

BRACE, BRACE

World leaders have agreed on a warning signal, in case Earth is on track to hit something in space.

When the Sun disappeared, Earth flew off into space. Earth is travelling quickly and could hit other planets, rocks or stars. If we are heading for one of these, speakers will sound the words 'brace, brace'.

CARROT FARMERS:
FRIEND OR FOE?
we truly trust these

The Earth <u>orbits</u> the Sun at over 107,000 kilometres per hour. The Sun's <u>gravity</u> keeps Earth in orbit. If the Sun disappeared, Earth would fly off and could hit other things in space.

IMAGINE SWINGING A ROCK ON A PIECE OF STRING IN A CIRCLE AND LETTING GO, IT WOULD FLY OFF IN A STRAIGHT LINE.

Year 45020

Dear Diary,

Today might be the 1st of January, 45020. It's hard to tell, since years were based on how long it took Earth to orbit the Sun.

It's getting hotter.

Humans from the year 2020 lived above water. I wonder if it will get hot enough for me to go above the ocean...

The Sun is a star. If the Earth didn't hit anything while zooming through space, it would reach the nearest star in 43,000 years. Earth could start orbiting it and finally begin getting hotter again.

IF EARTH GOT HOTTER AGAIN, THERE'S A SMALL CHANCE THAT HUMANS COULD RETURN TO LAND.

IT STARTS WITH US

That's scary stuff, isn't it? Don't worry, the Sun's not going to disappear. But, we must be careful not to block it out. In some countries, humans have caused a type of air <u>pollution</u> called smog.

Smog can block out sunlight. We can create less smog by walking and riding bikes instead of driving in cars. We must look after our planet, so that we never have to live in a world without the Sun.

GLOSSARY

average	the typical and usual; not outside the ordinary
gravity	the force that pulls everything towards the centre of objects in space
herbivores	animals that eat plants, instead of other animals
hydrothermal vent	an opening in the ocean floor that heated water flows out of
omnivores	animals that eat both plants and other animals
orbits	travels around an object in space in a curved path
pollution	harmful and poisonous things being added to an environment
reflecting	bouncing back light
temperature	how hot or cold something is

INDEX

food 4–6, 10–11, 16–17
humans 15, 17, 20–21
hydrothermal vents 14–15, 17
light 6–7, 9, 11, 23
Moon 8–9

oceans 15, 20
planets 6–7, 9, 12–13, 15, 18–21, 23
plants 10–11, 17
smog 22–23